Guide to Effective Retail Merchandise Management

A Step by Step Guide to Merchandising in a Retail Store

MEIR LIRAZ

Published by BizMove
www.bizmove.com

ISBN: 1548373435

ISBN-13: 978-1548373436

Table of Contents

MEIR LIRAZ

1. Introduction

This guide concerns itself with retail merchandise management which involves:

what merchandise to carry in stock

how much to buy and stock of each item

how much selling space to give each item

what price to charge for each item

how to display, advertise and promote each item

Merchandise management is sometimes mistaken with merchandising. Merchandising refers to good in-store display and promotion of merchandise. Merchandise management, as described above, is much more, as will be seen in the discussion to follow.

2. Selection Of Merchandise

What merchandise should be carried in stock is basic to good merchandise management. For this reason, much thought and research must be given to selecting merchandise appropriate for your store. In initiating a new store, as well as during periodic merchandise reviews in an established store, you need to think about your market. What are the people like, who shop in your area? Are they young married with children, or elderly couples, blue or white collar, high or low income? What are their leisure activities, and wants and needs, etc.? Each of these factors has impact upon the type of merchandise you would select.

Other ways for obtaining ideas for merchandise selection include:

Studying other stores in the area, watching closely the merchandise they do and do not offer. Determining whether merchandise not offered may have potential.

Obtaining suggestions from salespeople in similar stores.

Carefully listening and speaking to customers in general about what they like about other stores.

Reading the trade literature.

Following advertisements of chains and department stores.

In general, knowing your customers and their needs is crucial in merchandise selection.

In a more specific way you select merchandise with the use

of the tools for merchandise management discussed later in this section.

Generally, if a store is to be successful, sales and inventory should be reviewed periodically to:

See how many units of an item should be stocked and how much space should be given to them

Determine what should be done about slow moving items in inventory, and

Lay plans for sales, promotions and selection of new merchandise.

Two basic tools of merchandise management, which can help to determine how much of an item should be carried in stock, use gross profit as a basis for the calculations. They are:

Gross profit per square foot (or, profit/sq. ft.), and

Gross profit on investment (or, profit/investment)

Both of these tools help determine the average inventory which will bring the highest profit for each item. Once you understand them thoroughly, you can use a simpler tool, called stockturn. When applied properly, it can often replace the more cumbersome calculations.

3. Gross Profit

Since the two basic tools are built on gross profit, you need a clear view of the meaning of gross profit.

In a retail store, gross profit is the difference between what you pay for merchandise and what you sell it for.

There are two ways of calculating gross profit.

1. The simplest way is to take the selling price and subtract the cost.

Selling Price (-) Cost (=) Gross Profit

2. In a retail store, customers often return merchandise, some of which then has to be sold at less than full price. There are also frequent sales. Accountants and many retailers therefore prefer to calculate gross profit by subtracting the cost of merchandise from net sales. Net sales means total sales (as rung up on the register) less returns. Cost of merchandise, again, is what the store paid for the units which were sold but not returned.

Gross profit can be calculated as shown:

Total Sales (-) Return (-) Cost of Merchandise (=) Gross Profit

Example: Gross Profit

A retailer buys merchandise for $10 and sells that merchandise for $20. If the retailer sells 1,000 units but accepts 100 units in returns, what is her or his gross profit?

Using the formula above, gross profit can be calculated as follows:

$20,000 Total Sales (-) $ 2,000 For 100 Returns (-) $ 9,000 Cost of Net Merchandise Sold

(=) $ 9,000 Gross Profit

The same answer can also be obtained using the simpler formula: Since the gross profit on each unit is $10 ($20 selling price$10 cost), and 900 units were sold (and not returned), the gross profit on the merchandise is ($10 x 900 units) or $9,000 - the same as above. In reality, this second calculation may not be as simple because there may have been a special price sale and therefore a different selling price for some of the units.

Please note that expenses such as rent on your store, utilities, cost of labor, and other operating costs are paid out of gross profit. The amount remaining after such expenses are paid is your net profit. Obviously, the higher your gross profit the higher your net profit will be. This is because most of a retail store's operating expenses are fixed and do not increase significantly with greater sales.

Also note that gross profit is arrived at by using the cost of the specific merchandise which was actually sold - not your purchases for the same period.

4. Profit Per Square Foot

Profit per square foot provides an indication of how much profit an item of merchandise brings from each square foot of selling space it occupies. It therefore helps to determine how much space should be allocated to each item. Since floor and shelf space in a store is limited, profit/sq. ft. can be used to help you make the best use of your space.

As the term suggests, profit/sq. ft. is calculated by dividing the gross profit of an item by the area of selling space for that item. The formula is shown below:

Profit per Square Foot =

Gross Profit

_____

Sq. ft. of selling space

Example: Profit per Square Foot

Assume a retailer's business made $4,000 in gross profit last year on a particular line "x". The selling area for the line was 200 square feet of shelf and floor space. What is the profit per square foot on line 'x'?

Using the formula above, the profit per square foot on line "x" can be figured as follows:

Profit per Sq. Ft. =

$$\frac{\$4{,}000 \text{ gross profit on line "x"}}{200 \text{ sq. ft. of selling area for item "x"}} = \$20$$

5. Allocation of Space Based on Profit Per Square Foot

To get the highest profit from your available selling space, you must study each of your lines and items to determine which give you the highest, as well as the lowest, profit per square foot. To do this, calculate the profit/sq. ft. on some of your best moving items, and on some you consider least profitable. This will provide you with your profitability range and, using that range you can decide on the amount of gross profit you want each square foot in the store to bring you.

You can then increase overall profitability by taking action on low profit items. This can be done by:

Promoting them more effectively

Reducing space allotted to them, or

Replacing them

If all items, even the poorest, are yielding a sufficiently high profit/sq. ft. but you would like to increase profitability further, you can achieve that by:

Increasing promotion and merchandising efforts on items

Expanding the store, or

Both

This raises the question:

"What is the lowest gross profit/sq. ft. that the poorest

items should bring?"

This is not easy to answer. Every retail business has to carry some items which customers expect to find in the store, even if they are not profitable at all. That is why many retailers talk about "loss leaders". These low profit items, some of which may have to be sold at a net loss at certain times, should not be considered in the same manner as regular merchandise.

Every item of regular merchandise must bring a net profit (after all expenses have been paid). To determine what net profit an item or line will bring, you can calculate your expenses per square foot of selling space and subtract them from the gross profit per square foot to obtain the net profit per square foot for that item or line.

Gross profit per square foot (-) expenses per square foot (=) net profit per square foot

Expenses include salaries for employees, rent, insurance, packing materials, cleaning services, interest on loans, utilities, and other similar expenses as well as a fair salary for you. The sum of these costs are referred to as expenses per square foot.

For example, if all your expenses add up to $48,000 per year and you have 4000 square feet of selling space, then your expenses per square foot are $12.00, Any item or line which brings an annual gross profit per square foot (profit/sq. ft.) of less than $12.00 is not bringing you any net profit at all. In fact it is not paying its way and you should either promote it more effectively, or seriously consider replacing it with more profitable merchandise.

On-The-Job Activity 1

This activity consists of two parts. In Part A you will calculate your costs per square foot and in Part B you will determine your gross and net profits per square foot for several items.

Part A

To gain some direct use in the topics discussed, calculate your expenses per square foot of selling space. This will require you to:

1. Either add up all your expenses from the previous year (or from several months, and calculate the annual costs), or ask your accountant to give you this figure..

2. Measure all your usable selling space where merchandise is kept - the shelves, the floor space underneath racks, the floor space where merchandise is displayed, etc. Do not include storage space in the back room - only space on the selling floor.

3. Divide the square feet of selling space into the annual expenses to give you the expenses per square foot.

Part B

Select several items which you believe bring you a nice profit and two or three which you feel are not very profitable. Calculate both gross profit per square foot and net profit per square foot.

If possible, discuss the results of your work with a person knowledgeable in this area; pursue any ideas which may arise as a result of this discussion.

6. Gross Profit On Investment

In most cases profit/sq. ft. (gross profit per square foot) is adequate to determine how much space to allow to an item or line. However, there is one group of items or lines where looking at profit/ sq. ft. may not be adequate to decide whether the item or line is profitable. This is the case with relatively small, or average sized merchandise in which cost per unit is much higher than for most other merchandise. For this type of merchandise you also have to look at gross profit per dollar of investment (profit/ investment). This means that for these items you should allocate space as with other items on the basis of profit/sq. ft., but you also must keep your inventory as low as possible to assure best profit/investment.

If all your merchandise is fairly similar in cost per unit, and the units are all of fairly similar size then you do not have to be concerned with profit/investment. If, however, you have some small or average sized items or lines where the cost is high in comparison to your other merchandise, then it may be worthwhile to pay special attention to them.

Gross profit on investment (profit/investment) is the gross profit made on every dollar invested in average inventory of a merchandise item or line. It therefore provides a way of determining how many units to keep in inventory.

Profit/investment is found by dividing the annual gross profit brought by an item, by the dollar amount invested in the average inventory of that item.

Profit / investment =

Gross Profit

_____

$ Investment in average inventory

Investment in average inventory is determined by multiplying the number of units of average inventory, by the cost of a unit. Average inventory is the midpoint between the highest inventory, which occurs right after a new shipment is received, and the lowest inventory, which usually exists just before the new shipment arrives.

Example: Gross Profit on Investment (Profit / Investment)

Assume that a retailer sells $16,000 of a line of desk lamps each year The retailer purchases 100 units about once every 3 months for $20, each, and prices them at $40. If there are usually about 10 lamps left over when the new shipment arrives, then the retailer has $2200 invested in desk lamps, at the peak. When inventory is at its lowest about $200 are invested in these lamps. What is the retailer's annual gross profit and profit/investment? Gross profit can easily be found from the formula:

Total Sales=	$16,000
(-) Returns	0
(-) cost of merchandise sold and not returned	
(100 units x $20/unit x 4 times a years)	$ 8000
	_____
Annual gross profit from desk lamps	$ 8000

The retailer's investment in average inventory is the midpoint between $2200 (peak period) and $200 (low period). The midpoint is then obtained by adding the high and low figures and dividing by 2. In this example the midpoint is $1200; that is:

$$\frac{\$2200 + \$200}{2} = \frac{\$2400}{2} = \$1200$$

Average inventory investment in desk lamps = $1200

The profit/investment can then be calculated from the formula, shown before, as follows:

Profit / investment =

$$\frac{\$8000 \text{ gross profit on lamps}}{\$1200 \text{ Invested in average inventory}} \quad \$6.66$$

This means that an annual gross profit of $6.66 is made on every dollar invested in average inventory of this line of desk lamps.

7. Determining Inventory on Basis of Gross Profit on Investment profit / investment

To reiterate, items or merchandise lines which are small or average size and have high cost per unit should be given selling space the same way as other items - based on the profit/sq. ft. However, with this type, inventory must be carefully watched to bring the profit/investment as close as possible to that of other merchandise.

Probably the easiest way to do this is to calculate profit/investment (using the formula shown above) for several of the regular merchandise items; i.e., some with average profit/sq. ft. and some with high profit/sq. ft. This provides you with a range of desirable profit/investment figures.

This range can then become the goal for the high investment (high cost per unit) items. Simple actions to improve profitability of this type of merchandise are:

Promote more effectively.

Reduce average inventory by buying smaller quantities more frequently (if possible without increasing unit cost).

Obtain longer credit terms from the supplier (pay later so your investment is reduced by sales made from the time you received the shipment to the date when you pay for it).

If the profit/investment is very poor, replace the item or line with a more profitable one.

To decide when the profit/investment is so low that an item should be replaced you can:

Determine whether the money now invested in average inventory of an item elsewhere can be more profitably utilized within your business.

Ask your accountant to determine your total expenses (including your salary) per dollar invested in the entire inventory. If you subtract that number from the gross profit on investment (profit/investment) you obtain net profit per dollar investment. This net profit on investment should be at least equal to the cents per dollar you pay your bank for a loan. If it is not, you should seriously consider whether the item or line should be replaced.

On-The-Job Activity 2

To see how profit/investment can be useful in your business:

a. Select a few items that are small or average sized and have high cost compared to other merchandise in your store. Then calculate the profit on investment for these items, using the formula shown above.

b. Select one or two very profitable items and one or two items of average profit/sq. ft. from the other merchandise. Calculate the profit/investment for these items.

c. Compare profit/investment of the high cost items with the profit/investment you obtain from the other items and, if the difference is very great, calculate the net profit on investment (as discussed above) for the least profitable of the high cost items.

d. Decide what to do about any low profit/investment items.

8. Stockturn

Stockturn refers to the number of times the average inventory of a product has been sold. For example, if a retailer selling ball point pens has a stockturn of 5, it simply means that he or she sold 5 times the average inventory of that item over the period. There are two simple formulae for stockturn:

Knowing the stockturn of inventory allows you to adjust the level of your inventory and assure a desirable profit.

1. Stockturn =

$$\frac{\text{Number of units sold}}{\text{Average number of units carried in stock}} \text{ or,}$$

2. Stockturn =

$$\frac{\text{Dollar sales of item for the period}}{\text{Value of average stock of the item (At selling price)}}$$

Stockturn is usually expressed in terms of an annual figure and can be calculated by completing the formula above.

Note that stockturn and profit on investment are similar

Stockturn =

$$\frac{\text{Dollar sales of items for the period (net sales)}}{\text{Value of average inventory (at selling price)}}$$

while:

Profit on investment =

Gross profit

Value of average inventory (at cost)

Example: Stockturn

Assume that a certain retailer who sells $25.00 watches orders monthly about 20 watches ($500). When the shipment arrives, the stock has usually dropped to about 10 watches ($250).

Assume that there are no seasonal fluctuations. What is the stockturn on the watches?

Since stockturn =

Net sales (annual)

Average inventory

Net sales are 20 units x 12 months or 240 units - equivalent to $6000 of sales.

Average inventory is the midpoint between 10 watches (just prior to arrival of shipment) and 30 watches (following shipment arrival) - or 20 watches; they are worth $500 at retail price.

Stockturn =

240 watches sold

--- = 12, or

20 watches in average inventory

Stockturn =

$6000 net sales

$$\frac{\text{\$6000 net sales}}{\text{\$500 average inventory}} = 12$$

$500 average inventory

This simply means that the average inventory of watches has been sold 12 times over the year.

Once you know what profit/sq. ft. you want on your regular merchandise and on your high cost items, then you can calculate the stockturn you need for these different types of items. The stockturn figure then becomes a shorthand way to decide on quantity to buy and quantity to keep in inventory.

9. Using Profit/Investment, Profit/Sq. Ft. and Stockturns

Now that you know how to calculate profit/sq. ft., profit/investment and stockturn, you can apply them to improve the profitability of your store.

These three concepts each have a useful place.

Gross profit per square foot (profit/sq. ft.) can help you decide how much space to give to an item or merchandise line. If you find the items giving you the best profit/sq. ft. you have a goal to attain in giving space to other items. Furthermore, if you calculate your expenses per square foot, you can also determine which of your lowest profit items are being carried at a loss, thereby allowing you to rectify the situation.

Profit on investment can serve as a check for your high cost items to tell you which are very profitable and which require so high an investment in inventory that you should question whether they are worth carrying.

Stockturn is an easy way to decide how much to order, especially of staple items.

Once you have calculated the stockturns for several profitable items, you can use the stockturn

10. Implementing A Merchandise Improvement Program

Utilizing the tools discussed previously in this section, you could improve the profit you obtain from the lines you carry by:

Mentally separating your merchandise into a few categories based on size and cost.

For each category, selecting those items which you consider to be your best products; and determining the stockturn for these.

Selecting a few of what you consider to be your poorest products; calculate their stockturns.

Selecting a stockturn figure that you could use as your goal for all merchandise in a given category, based on what you found the stockturns to be for both your best and your poorest products.

Keeping the desired stockturns in mind as you purchase new merchandise in various categories, and gradually bringing your entire stock closer to the turns set for each category.

Obviously, stockturns are only general guidelines. There are many reasons why, with respect to a specific item, you may not be able to adhere to them:

You may have to purchase minimum quantities of an item so that you might not be able to reduce your average inventory enough to maintain the stockturns you have selected.

You may have an opportunity to obtain quantity discounts on large volume purchases. In cases where it pays to take the discount, your stockturns would also probably be smaller than the stockturns you have set.

Stockturns alone are not enough of a guide upon which to evaluate your merchandise. In order to decide which merchandise may not be appropriate for your store and which should be replaced by more profitable merchandise, you should also look at the profit/ sq. ft. and profit on investment for the poorest items in each category, as discussed earlier in this section.

Before you decide to replace items from your merchandise lines which show poor performance in terms of profit/sq. ft. or profit on investment, you should assure yourself that your manner of merchandising them isn't the problem. In many instances, products can be promoted in order to improve their volume. With these items, you must try various advertising and promotion strategies as will later be discussed. At other times, it is obvious that little can be done with a product. Some items just do not lend themselves well to advertising or to promotion. In such cases gradual replacement is the best strategy.

11. Gradual Replacement of Undesirable Merchandise

Although it is possible to simply drop a low profit item from inventory, such a procedure narrows selection and may leave gaps of space within your store. It is generally better to first locate replacement merchandise before phasing out undesirable products. This is especially true where an entire merchandise line is involved, since simply dropping the line would create lower overall volume and less sales with which to carry your fixed costs.

Replacement of an undesirable product begins with a search for merchandise that might be useful in your store. Such a search can include steps used to initially decide on the merchandise lines to carry. You might:

Look at what competitors in similar stores offer.

Obtain suggestions from sales people.

Carefully listen to customers about the kind of things they are looking for; talk to customers about what they like in other stores.

Carefully read the trade literature.

Look at the advertisements in chain stores and department stores.

By remaining alert and using these methods, you will gradually acquire new items to carry in your store and will be able to see whether these items improve your profitability. Sometimes entire lines of merchandise can be added this way.

Once you have introduced a new product or line, you must support it with:

In-store promotions

Advertising

Sales efforts

Customers first must be aware that the line can be purchased in your store before it will become profitable for you. It is only after all sales and promotional efforts fail that it is probably best to mark dawn and sell remaining items and start again with a different item.

This is a gradual and difficult process, of course, but if you persevere, continue to identify those items that are least desirable, and slowly attempt to replace them, gradually the profitability of your store is certain to improve.

12. Checklist For Improving The Merchandise Mix In Your Store

This checklist is not designed to be exhaustive or to provide you with all the answers on how to improve merchandise selection and profitability of your store. It can, however, provide you with a starting point and a number of ideas which you may wish to consider for merchandise improvement.

Classify your merchandise into categories based on size and cost.

Determine which products appear to be the best and least desirable products in each category.

Set reasonable stockturns for each category.

Work gradually toward an inventory position which will bring equal turns on all merchandise items and lines within each category.

Determine what profit/sq. ft. the poorest items of each category bring.

Determine which of your least desirable items might be made more attractive through in-store promotion, and which items are less promising and need to be replaced or eliminated.

Hold sales on all the items which should be eliminated.

Advertise and promote those items that appear to have some promise in becoming more profitable.

Experiment with new products which may be able to replace your least desirable merchandise.

Evaluate the results of advertising and promotion to see whether the additional products should be replaced.

Find new products to take their place.

Try advertising and promoting those new products to see whether they are any better.

Strive to gradually develop an improved line of merchandise.

13. Retail Pricing, Sales And Markdowns

Price, in some industries, has a great deal of impact on sales volume. Once customers are familiar with a product and know what they want, they often tend to buy for price. When this is the case, it is necessary to run sales frequently and to advertise them, so that customers know your store is a good place to frequent if they want to save money. In this environment, all prices have to be watched carefully with those of competitors. In other businesses, pricing is less sensitive and normal markup can be figured on most products.

It is often possible to attract more customers to your store and sell more merchandise if your prices on some items are somewhat lower than those of your competitors. For other merchandise, especially that which is less competitive and more unique to your store, you may have to set a higher selling price, since you may not get the volume of sales you need in order to make a good profit. In trying to decide on a price, it is useful to experiment first with different prices.

For example, if you are selling 75 units per week at $1.60 gross profit per unit, your total weekly profit is $120. This is the equivalent of selling 100 units at $1.20 each.

In this example then, a retailer may offer a product for sale at a $0.40 savings to the consumer but still earn the same weekly gross profit if he or she is able to sell only 25 more units at the lower price.

On The Job Activity

In your own business, select one or two products and post a "sale" price in the window or on the item. Reduce your profit by about 1/4 and keep that lower price for at least one month. Then check whether your total profit was higher than previously at the old price for the same time period.

If possible, discuss your thoughts with a person knowledgeable in the area of merchandise management; determine other experiments in pricing which may be worthwhile in your particular situation.

14. Sales and Markdowns

Basically, there are three occasions for holding sales:

Start of season sales may be run to introduce the consumer to new merchandise. Often, it is useful to run pre-season sales to get a jump on competitors. Such sales before the season tend to take sales away from competitors.

Holiday sales are always effective due to the large number of people available for shopping and in the market for gifts.

Sales to clean out merchandise are perhaps least frequently held but should be held more often. Marking down least desirable merchandise along with end of season merchandise will not only remove slow moving products from your inventory, but will also provide you with cash-on-hand necessary to replenish inventory with new and more profitable merchandise.

Additionally, frequent sales get you into the eye of the consumer more often. Sales attract greater numbers of people into stores and, more often than not, such people will also come in to buy regular merchandise too. Even selling merchandise at cost usually entails no loss, since you will be able to replace empty store space with better moving merchandise, thereby attracting more people into the store.

15. Retail Advertising And Promotion

Two approaches may be used to increase both customer traffic in your store and the sale of specific items or merchandise lines. These approaches, best used in conjunction with each other, are:

Advertising - which addresses those potential customers who are not within the store

In-store promotions - which can attract the attention of customers within the store or via window displays

Advertising

Although the primary purpose of this section is to discuss merchandise management, advertising is so important to the concept that its inclusion, though brief, is necessary.

There are two major types of advertising:

Advertising to acquaint potential buyers with the special features of a product. With many industries, advertising of this type is done by the manufacturer of the product. Quite often, however, the retailer must do some of this advertising. When this occurs, it is often necessary to work with an advertising agency so they may help you write the copy (wording) such that the advertising will bring the best results. Such advertising concentrates almost solely on the single featured product.

Advertising the availability and price of nationally known merchandise. Much retail advertising is merely directed at letting potential customers know that the product is available and informing the customer of special prices or promotions which may encourage her/him to buy, at your store. This is perhaps best done through 'Omnibus' ads which feature many products, their prices, and brief slogans about their benefits. Consumers very often "shop" such ads and will come into your store to buy one or two of the items listed. While there, they buy other things on impulse.

Whatever your message may be, there are many ways to advertise - depending on how much information you wish to impart to prospective consumers, what kind of information (audio and/or visual), and how many consumers you wish to reach.

Retailers who cater to local clientele may use advertising methods such as:

In-house flyers indicating products and bargains

Signs both internal and external to the store

Informative in-house displays of merchandise

Direct mail advertising

Local newspapers

Distribution of flyers by hand or using the local newspaper deliveries (some papers have such arrangements)

Those retailers who wish to launch a large scale campaign may, of course, resort to advertising via radio, television, or widely circulated newspapers.

It is very important to remember that for any kind of

advertising, single ads bring very sparse results. In order to make an advertising campaign successful, it is usually necessary to advertise repeatedly (five or six times during a one to two week period) to acquaint consumers with your service or product and, most important, with your store. It is also necessary to maintain a regular program of advertising throughout the year in order to continue bringing customers into the store.

Continual experimentation is necessary to determine which approaches are best. Although proper advertising may involve an initially high expense, if it succeeds both in drawing more clientele into your store and in increasing sales in both advertised and unadvertised products, the initial investment may more than pay for itself.

Once advertising has brought the consumer into your store, promotion and sales efforts must transfer the customer's attention and interest into desire and action to buy.

In-Store Promotion

Promoting merchandise may often be achieved by special arrangements with a manufacturer or a wholesaler. Often new merchandise will be offered at low introductory prices and the manufacturer or wholesaler will provide the retailer with special informative displays of the product as well as offer special rewards to the consumer.

Many times a manufacturer will not offer displays but you will want to promote certain merchandise nevertheless. Basic ways through which you may create your own in-store promotions are:

window displays

special in-store displays

signs and posters

personal selling efforts

Displays

Both in-house displays of merchandise and advertising displays should be:

attention getting in coloration and layout

informative in regard to the product

either a direct or subtle sales pitch to convince the customer that he or she needs the product

informative of price, especially if it is a 'special price'

Both display advertising and in-house displays often do well to feature a number of related products, some of which may or may not be on sale.

Past studies in advertising have shown that a person's eye is generally attracted to the center of a display, then off to the right of center and lastly reaches the edge of the display. It is therefore good practice to place a featured item, which may be on sale, at the center of the display and another product for which you most wish to generate sales, to the immediate right of the featured item. Other related products may be placed outward from around the center of the display.

When creating a display, it is important to tie-in merchandise lines with one another wherever possible. In this way, customers who are in the market for a specific product are also exposed to many related products and accessories which they will often buy. Such tie-in displays also create a more organized appearance of your store and will make products easier to find. For example, a person looking for toothpaste might be more likely to buy a toothbrush, dental floss, or mouthwash if those products are in close proximity to the toothpaste.

Tie-in displays also help to generate impulse buying. Quite often an advertised or 'sale' product will draw people into the store who will buy not only the advertised product but will also buy, on impulse, other unadvertised merchandise. Sales are often helpful to impulse buying since, when people feel they are getting a good bargain, they are often likely to reciprocate by purchasing other merchandise from you with money saved from the sale.

Sales Effort

All promotions and attempts to interest customers in new lines, new products, or in special sales, will work better if they are supported with sales effort. For example, just before a product is rung up at the cash register, it is always a good idea to ask a customer whether he or she knows of a special sale, knows of a special product you are promoting, or could use something that goes well with the things the customer has already purchased.

If such reminders are given in a friendly way without being persistent, many customers will make additional inquiries and often additional purchases.

On-The-Job Activity

For your next in-store promotion, you might try using a tie-in display, with the featured item in the center of the display, surrounded by related products or accessories.

If possible, discuss your ideas with a person knowledgeable in advertising; pursue any additional ideas which may arise from such a discussion.

www.ingramcontent.com/pod-product-compliance
Lightning Source LLC
Chambersburg PA
CBHW051300170526
45165CB00004B/1788